University of Charleston Library
Charleston, WV 25304

CONTENTS

RESPONSIBILITY FOR CED PROGRAM STATEMENTS

The publication of this statement is authorized by the regulations of the Research and Policy Committee that empower the Program Committee to issue statements within the framework of the policies previously stated by the Research and Policy Committee.

This statement represents the views of the members of the Program Committee. The proposals are not necessarily endorsed by other Trustees of CED or by the advisors, contributors, staff members, or others associated with CED.

Library of Congress Cataloging-in-Publication Data

Committee for Economic Development.
    Connecting inner-city youth to the world of work : a program
  statement   / by the Committee for Economic Development.
      p.   cm.

    Includes bibliographical references
    ISBN 0-87186-125-9 (alk. paper)
    1. Career education — United States.   2. School-to-work transition —
United States.   3. Economic development — Effect of education on.
LC1037.5.C65   1997
370.11'3' — dc21   97-13964
                                               CIP

First printing in bound-book form: 1997
Paperback: $12.00
Printed in the United States of America
Design: Rowe & Ballantine

COMMITTEE FOR ECONOMIC DEVELOPMENT
477 Madison Avenue, New York, N.Y. 10022
(212) 688-2063

2000 L Street, N.W., Suite 700, Washington, D.C. 20036
(202) 296-5860

http://www.ced.org

PROGRAM COMMITTEE

---

*Voted to approve the program statement but submitted memoranda of comment, reservation, or dissent. See page 31.

PREFACE

For more than two decades, the Committee for Economic Development (CED) has been deeply involved in the interrelated issues of America's work force, its educational system, and its distressed urban areas. Our positions have been articulated in such policy statements as *American Workers and Economic Change* (1996), *Rebuilding Inner-City Communities* (1995), *Connecting Students to a Changing World* (1995), *Putting Learning First* (1994), *The Unfinished Agenda* (1991), *An America that Works* (1990), *Children in Need* (1987), *Work and Change* (1987), *Investing in Our Children* (1985), *Jobs for the Hard-to-Employ* (1978), *Education for the Urban Disadvantaged* (1971), and *Training and Jobs for the Urban Poor* (1970).

Connecting Inner-City Youth to the World of Work applies policy positions developed in those earlier statements to a special topic: improving opportunities for young people growing up in the nation's poorest urban neighborhoods to join and prosper in the mainstream American workplace.

CED appreciates the generosity and vision of the Metropolitan Life Foundation in supporting the preparation of this statement and sponsoring a CED/MetLife symposium on this subject in Washington, D.C., on December 5, 1995. Signaling the keen interest of the business community, the keynote address at that symposium was delivered by Harry P. Kamen, Chairman, President and Chief Executive Officer of the Metropolitan Life Insurance Company.

CED is also pleased to acknowledge the contributions of Sandra Kessler Hamburg, CED Vice President and Director of Education and Special Projects, in organizing the symposium and Marc Bendick, Jr., of Bendick and Egan Economic Consultants, Inc., in drafting this program statement.

Josh S. Weston
Chairman
CED Program Committee

EXECUTIVE SUMMARY

The United States should provide opportunities for all young persons entering its work force to develop productive careers. But the nation's schools fail to equip many of our youth with appropriate skills; the job market often fails to link them to long-term, advancement-oriented employment; and their communities often provide few role models of adult employment success.

These problems are particularly acute in severely distressed neighborhoods in the nation's large cities. To create a more favorable environment for education and employment in these communities, CED has stressed the importance of:

- Prenatal and postnatal health care, parenting education, and developmentally oriented preschool programs so that disadvantaged children begin school ready to learn

- Health and social services for students and their families to address problems that hamper learning and distract schools from their educational mission

- Initiatives to control guns and drugs that disrupt learning and community life

- Enhancement of role models exemplifying stable employment and other constructive behavior

- Participation by parents and neighborhood institutions in educational, employment, and other community development initiatives

Although the inner-city environment makes the preparation of young people for work especially difficult, deficiencies in the nation's work-preparatory efforts also affect middle-class youth in suburban communities. To strengthen elementary and secondary schools across the nation, CED advocates:

- Establishing higher educational standards, including enhanced expectations for academic achievement and increased rigor in curricula

- Improving the quality of teachers through requirements for mastery of the subjects they teach, incentives linking compensation to performance, and flexibility to recruit excellent candidates who lack standard teaching credentials

- Increasing schools' use of information technology, integrating classroom use of computers throughout the curriculum, and providing greater access to the National Information Infrastructure for both students and teachers

- Strengthening school-based management by defining and rewarding performance and allocating more authority and responsibility to principals, teachers, parents, and students

- Expanding charter schools and public school choice to increase educational alternatives and competitive incentives for school performance

To improve the work preparation provided by schools, these reforms in educational management must be accompanied by changes in the style of teaching and learning in the nation's classrooms. Underlying the disconnection between youth and career employment is a more fundamental disconnection between the nation's educational system and the world of work. Innovative schools are making *contextualized learning* central to their teaching and using the work place as a learning context. This approach should become widely adopted in schools across the nation, and federal and state policymakers need to continue and expand their support of such educational reforms.

Employers can more effectively utilize the graduates of these improved schools if they modify employment practices affecting young job applicants and entry-level employees. In particular, employers need to take the following actions:

- Increase recruiting through inner-city schools and other community-based sources of job referrals

- Provide student internships and similar opportunities for inner-city job seekers to demonstrate performance on the job

- Expand public advertising of employment vacancies

- Use school transcripts and teacher recommendations when making hiring decisions

- Reward entry-level workers for educational achievement and skills even when these credentials are more relevant to future duties than current ones

- Expand "diversity management" initiatives to enhance the retention and productivity of employees of diverse demographic backgrounds

- Enhance upward-mobility opportunities for employees who invest in education while employed

- Redesign career ladders to provide workers with initial access at younger ages

- Expand the range of occupations in which apprenticeships and similar arrangements offer formal paths of upward mobility

By such means, schools, entry-level employment, and long-term careers can be linked for residents of inner cities and all the nation's younger workers.

INTRODUCTION

A skilled, productive work force is essential to the economic growth and international competitiveness of the United States. Failure to utilize our nation's diverse labor force means lost national output. At the same time, it leaves workers struggling to earn wages that enable them to support themselves and a family. The nation can ill afford the consequences, from costly welfare dependency to skyrocketing prison populations, when the job market fails to absorb all segments of the population effectively. To ensure both prosperity and social progress, the United States must extend opportunities to develop productive careers to *all* young persons entering its labor market.

Despite this aspiration, the nation's schools today too often fail to provide our youth with the skills prerequisite to productive employment, and the nation's system for job placement too often fails to link them to career-oriented jobs. Some communities offer inadequate role models of employment success to guide young people toward productive careers. As a result, significant numbers of younger Americans fail to get connected to the world of work.

Alarm about this situation has been sounded most vigorously with respect to minority and immigrant youth being educated in public schools in inner-city neighborhoods. For its work force, the United States is increasingly reliant on minorities, recent immigrants, and other groups traditionally outside the employment mainstream.[1] A large proportion of these workers grow up in the nation's central cities,[2] where schools and labor markets

---

1. *An America That Works: The Life-Cycle Approach to a Competitive Work Force* (New York: Committee for Economic Development, 1990), Chapter 2; *Workforce 2000* (Washington, D.C.: U.S. Department of Labor, 1987).

2. Nearly 40 percent of the nation's African American children, 32 percent of its Latino children, and 36 percent of its students with limited English proficiency are educated in only 47 large-city school districts. See *Rebuilding Inner-City Communities: A New Approach to the Nation's Urban Crisis* (New York: Committee for Economic Development, 1995), p. 2.

often serve them poorly. For example, a recent study of the District of Columbia's public schools lamented high school dropout rates exceeding 50 percent, scores on the Comprehensive Test of Basic Skills averaging 36 percent below national norms, fewer than half of graduates in vocational fields (such as cosmetology) passing licensing examinations, and fewer than 70 percent of student interns rated by work supervisors as meeting their company's minimum hiring standards. Six months after graduation, 63 percent of the city's high school graduates were unemployed.[3]

DISCONNECTIONS BETWEEN YOUTH AND WORK

When young workers become discouraged by labor market prospects as poor as that 63 percent figure symbolizes, one form that the disconnection between them and the world of work can take is withdrawal. Instead of becoming employees, young people can become welfare dependents, prison inmates, or idle labor force dropouts. In 1994, among persons age 25 to 64 without high school diplomas, only 58.3 percent were in the nation's work force, compared with 77.8 percent of high school graduates. That difference in labor force participation alone corresponds to 6.9 million workers — and perhaps $177 billion in national income per year — "missing" from the American economy.[4]

But lost national output is only part of the cost. In a book chapter aptly titled "The High Costs of Rotten Outcomes," Lisbeth Schorr reminds us of the huge public outlays triggered, in no small part, when people do not earn their own living. Federal, state, and local public expenditures in 1992 included $208 billion in public assistance payments and $79.5 billion in expenditures for police protection and corrections.[5] Although better labor market opportunities would not eliminate all these expenditures, they could reduce them substantially.

3. *Linking Learning with Earning* (Washington, D.C: District of Columbia Public Schools, 1992), p. 5. According to another survey, half of the students in the nation's large-city public schools leave before high school graduation, the majority fall behind the national average in reading in the fourth grade and never catch up, and in some large-city schools, only one-third of graduates score well enough on military qualifying tests to be allowed to enlist; See Paul Hill, "Urban Education," in *Urban America: Policy Choices for America,* ed. James Steinberg, David W. Lyon, and Mary E. Vaiana (Santa Monica, Calif.: RAND, 1992), p. 110.

4. *Statistical Abstract of the United States* (Washington D.C.: U.S. Department of Commerce, 1995), Tables 630 and 705. These estimates assume that each "missing" worker would produce half as much national income per year as the average member of the civilian labor force.

5. Lisbeth Schorr, *Within Our Reach, Breaking the Cycle of Disadvantage* (New York: Doubleday, 1988), Chapter 1; *Statistical Abstract,* Tables 333 and 585.

A second form of disconnection between youth and work is *underemployment* — young people who are employed, but only in poorly paid, short-term, dead-end jobs. A worker employed full-time throughout the year at the federal minimum wage of $4.75 per hour earns only $9,880 a year. Over the past 15 years, the proportion of jobs in the American economy paying below the federal poverty level has increased from 12 percent to 16 percent, currently employing 21 million American workers.[6] Over the same years, the average time between job changes for less educated workers has fallen significantly.[7]

Of course, minimum-wage, short-term employment can be a useful starting point for workers with little prior experience and limited qualifications. Entry-level positions can provide an initial orientation to the world of work, marketable skills, and job contacts. But not all entry-level jobs offer such long-term benefits. According to one estimate, more than 35 percent of male high school graduates in the American labor market have still not moved from short-term, entry-level positions to stable employment by their early thirties.[8]

Even workers who eventually obtain well-compensated, career-oriented employment often find the process of connecting to those opportunities unnecessarily turbulent, prolonged, and inefficient. Many young people require a period of maturing after high school before they are ready to take advantage of high-quality job opportunities. Correspondingly, many employers do not hire workers for career-oriented jobs until they are in their mid-twenties. However, the intervening period can be spent aimlessly or productively. When students leave school without goals and their initial jobs do little to develop in them a sense of purpose, the years following high school tend to become time lost rather than a time of maturing, preparing, and connecting.

When the "ideal" progression — from home to school to entry-level jobs to career employment — does not occur for a young worker, that per-

---

6. *American Workers and Economic Change* (New York: Committee for Economic Development, 1996), p. 33.

7. *American Workers and Economic Change*, p. 29.

8. Robert I. Lerman, "Building Hope, Skills, and Careers: Making a U.S. Youth Apprenticeship System," in Social Policies for Children, ed. Jennifer Hochschild, Irwin Garfinkel, and Sara McLanahan (Washington, D.C.: The Brookings Institution, 1996), p. 5. See also J. A. Klerman and L. A. Karoly, "Young Men and the Transition to Stable Employment," *Monthly Labor Review* 117 (August 1994); pp. 31-48, and John Tyler, Richard Murname, and Frank Levy, "Are More College Graduates Really Taking 'High School' Jobs?" *Monthly Labor Review* 133 (December 1995), pp. 18-27.

4

son sometimes becomes a client of "second chance" government employment and training programs, for example, those funded by the Job Training Partnership Act (JTPA) or welfare-to-work initiatives. Such efforts at remediation are typically far more expensive than prevention.[9] Worse, these remedial programs often do not produce substantial changes in participants' labor market prospects. The more successful public employment and training programs, such as some welfare-to-work programs targeting young women with little prior work experience, only break even in terms of cost-effectiveness; programs for disadvantaged young men tend to produce even fewer changes in participants' employment and earnings.[10] If schools fail to prepare their students for employment, later remedial programs cannot easily offset that failure.

SIMILAR PROBLEMS AMONG MIDDLE-CLASS YOUTH

Although the previous discussion emphasized the problems of young people growing up in distressed inner-city neighborhoods, concern about work force preparation extends to non-college-bound students from more affluent communities. In 1988, the Commission on the Skills of the American Workforce drew attention to the mismatch between the college-preparatory emphasis in the nation's high schools and the fact that half of high school graduates did not enroll in postsecondary education.[11] This theme was subsequently amplified by the Secretary of Labor's Commission on

9. For example, the Job Corps is a residential program for economically disadvantaged out-of-school youth that provides an intensive combination of remedial education, job skills training, and social services. These efforts are highly cost-effective, returning $1.45 in benefits for each $1.00 invested. However, the cost per trainee year is higher than the annual costs of attending an elite private college. See Laurie J. Bassi and Orley Ashenfelter, "Direct Job Creation and Job Training Programs," in *Fighting Poverty, What Works and What Doesn't*, ed. Sheldon Danziger and Daniel Weinberg (Cambridge, Mass.: Harvard University Press, 1986), p. 146.

10. Judith Gueron, Edward Pauley, and Cameran Laugy, *From Welfare to Work* (New York: Russell Sage Foundation, 1991); *What's Working (and What's Not), A Summary of Research on the Employment Impacts of Employment and Training Programs* (Washington, D.C.: U.S. Department of Labor, 1995); Larry Orr et al., *Does Training for the Disadvantaged Work? Evidence from the JTPA National Study* (Washington, D.C.: Urban Institute Press, 1996).

11. *The Forgotten Half: Pathways to Success for America's Youth and Young Families* (Washington, D.C.: Youth and America's Future, 1988). See also *America's Choice: High Skills or Low Wages!* (Rochester, N.Y.: National Center on Education and the Economy, 1990) and *A Nation at Risk: The Imperative for Educational Reform* (Washington, D.C.: U.S. Government Printing Office, 1983). By 1995, the proportion of high school graduates enrolling in postsecondary education had increased to 62 percent.

Achieving Necessary Skills (SCANS), which found much of the nation's work force inadequately prepared in literacy and numeracy, personal qualities such as honesty and responsibility, and workplace competencies such as the ability to work in teams, budget resources, seek information, and solve unstructured problems.[12] The General Accounting Office has estimated that more than one quarter of the nation's 33 million youth age 16 to 24 do not meet employer requirements for entry-level positions or command the academic skills expected of high school graduates; in a survey conducted in 1995, 316 companies reported that 43 percent of their new hires needed enhancement of their basic skills.[13]

The rapid acceleration of technological and structural change in the American economy enhances the urgency of this message. The rising skill requirements of jobs and the accelerating frequency of job changes render inadequate levels of educational achievement that once provided access to mainstream employment. In the 1990s, well-compensated careers for which high school graduation is sufficient preparation are rapidly becoming extinct.

During the 1980s and 1990s, American schools have made some progress in enhancing the skills of their students. Between 1982 and 1994, the nationwide proportion of 16 - to 24-year-olds dropping out prior to high school graduation fell from 13.9 percent to 10.5 percent; the proportion of high school graduates who had taken advanced subjects such as algebra, geometry, trigonometry, chemistry, and physics doubled; and the proportion of high school graduates going directly to postsecondary education increased from 51 percent to 62 percent.[14] Nevertheless, particularly in many inner-city schools, the pace of change in job requirements continues to outstrip improvements in educational achievement.

---

12. *Learning a Living: A Blueprint for High Performance* (Washington, D.C.: U.S. Department of Labor, 1992). See also A.P. Carnevale, L. Gainer, and A. Meltzer, *Workplace Basics: The Skills Employers Want* (San Francisco: Jossey-Bass, 1989).

13. *Training Strategies: Preparing Non-College Youth for Employment in the U.S. and Foreign Countries* (Washington, D.C.: U.S. General Accounting Office, 1990), p. 2; The Olsten Forum on Human Resource Issues and Trends, *Managing and Developing the New Work Force* (Melville, N.Y.: Olsten Corporation, 1995), p. 1. See also *An Assessment of American Education* (New York: Committee for Economic Development, 1991).

14. *American Workers and Economic Change,* p. 45. However, such changes in educational inputs do not always translate into enhanced learning. For example, increases in student mastery of science and mathematics may be more modest than enrollment increases in mathematics and science classes.

Summarizing the implications of these patterns in an economy of rapid technological change and intense international competition, CED recently concluded:

The new economy is generally good news for workers who have education beyond high school and preparation for careers in managerial, professional, and technical occupations. In most cases, opportunities and rewards for these workers will be further enhanced by experience with new technologies and continual training on the job. Those who are less prepared, however, are finding a very unwelcoming job market. . . . Higher skill requirements also have made entry-level jobs that provide a first rung on career ladders more difficult to obtain for the least skilled.[15]

15. *American Workers and Economic Change*, pp. 3-4.

STRENGTHENING COMMUNITY SUPPORT FOR EDUCATION AND EMPLOYMENT

How can young Americans be made beneficiaries rather than victims of this new economy?

The process of doing so cannot be restricted to school hours or school years. Educators cannot effectively prepare young people for work unless students arrive at school ready to learn; unless lessons are reinforced by families, neighbors, and peers; and unless employers welcome graduates — unless, in short, the community provides a system of institutions, attitudes, and processes that support the schools.

Unfortunately, in many inner-city neighborhoods, this system of support is dangerously weak. Some neighborhoods are heavily burdened with multiple problems, including crime and violence, welfare dependency and family instability, poverty and joblessness, physical blight and poor housing, and inadequate services and social isolation. The defining characteristic of a severely distressed neighborhood is that such problems coexist, reinforce each other, and jointly overwhelm the community's problem-solving resources.[16] In those circumstances, efforts to improve the performance of schools often founder under the adverse impact of other unresolved problems in the schools' communities.

Such circumstances are by no means typical of all urban neighborhoods or all minority-dominated neighborhoods. In fact, they characterize only about 11 percent of all census tracts within the 100 largest cities in the

---

16. *Rebuilding Inner-City Communities,* Chapter 2. Such destructive circumstances are sometimes diagnosed as deficiencies in *social capital,* the resources embedded in social relationships among persons and organizations that facilitate cooperation and collaboration in communities. The principal forms of social capital are information sharing; trust, based on expectations of reciprocal support; and norms, values, and social expectations that maintain social order.

nation.[17] Taken together, however, these multiple-problem neighborhoods are home to nearly 6 million persons, many of them students and young job seekers.

To create a more favorable environment for education and employment in these communities, CED has recommended action on a number of fronts. These recommendations include a willingness to increase selected public expenditures as an appropriate investment in the future of the American economy and American society.[18]

To ensure that disadvantaged children begin school ready to learn, CED believes that investments in young children throughout the preschool years are particularly important:

> It is less costly to society and to individuals to prevent early failures through efforts directed toward parents and children alike from prenatal care through age five. Such efforts should include: prenatal and postnatal care . . . and developmental screening; parenting education for both mothers and fathers . . . ; quality child-care arrangements for poor working parents that stress social development and school readiness; and quality preschool programs for all disadvantaged three- and four-year-olds.[19]

Disadvantaged students often need substantial health and social services. Students require stable personal circumstances to learn without handicaps or distractions. However, schools need to be relieved of the excessive responsibility for addressing such problems that have, de facto, fallen upon them. Accordingly, CED has called for health and social services for school-age children and their families to address problems that hamper learning and distract schools from their educational mission:

---

17. *Rebuilding Inner-City Communities*, p. 10. An additional 33 percent of census tracts in these 100 largest cities are at the margin of decline in both a social and a geographic sense and are likely to complete the process of decay if left unaided.

18. *Rebuilding Inner-City Communities*, p. 39.

19. *Children in Need, Investment Strategies for the Educationally Disadvantaged* (New York: Committee for Economic Development, 1987), p. 11. See also *The Unfinished Agenda, A New Vision for Child Development and Education* (New York: Committee for Economic Development, 1991), and Robert Haveman and Barbara Wolfe, *Succeeding Generations, On the Effect of Investments in Children* (New York: Russell Sage Foundation, 1994).

States and communities must lift the burden of addressing children's health and social needs from the backs of educators. They must, of course, arrange needed services for children and their families, often in collaboration with the schools. But other state and community agencies should pay for and provide these services so that schools can concentrate on their primary mission: learning and academic achievement.[20]

Nothing disrupts the educational and employment processes more than violence in students' homes, schools, and neighborhoods. CED believes that the easy availability of weapons for criminal purposes is a significant contributor to civil instability in inner-city neighborhoods and the fear-based separation between these neighborhoods and the broader society. Accordingly:

The most important precondition for community building that federal, state, and local governments can provide is to eliminate the national plague of cheap handguns and assault weapons and to take firearms out of the hands of juveniles and criminals. Such efforts have been enhanced by recent federal legislation mandating waiting periods for the purchase of weapons, banning selected assault weapons, and enhancing data systems tracking weapons purchases. At the federal, state, and local levels, such efforts should be continued through vigorous enforcement of existing gun control laws and expanded through legislation imposing substantially broader restrictions on weapons and ammunition.[21]

A second major disrupter of inner-city communities is the traffic in illegal drugs. This pernicious trade leaves shocking numbers of inner-city young people dead, scarred by criminal records, or addicted and unable to function as learners, earners, parents, or community members. CED

20. *Putting Learning First: Governing and Managing the Schools for High Achievement* (New York: Committee for Economic Development, 1994), p. 1; See also *Rebuilding Inner-City Communities*, pp. 30-31.

21. *Rebuilding Inner-City Communities*, p. 5.

believes that federal, state, and local governments must act decisively to reduce the adverse impact of illegal drugs on community life. However, many current efforts toward this end are not well crafted:

> Current antidrug efforts rely primarily on interdiction to prevent drugs entering the country and incarceration to deter drug distribution and abuse. These efforts do not effectively reduce the trade in illegal drugs in inner cities. . . . Federal, state, and local governments should shift resources from the current incarceration-oriented approach to preventing drug use through education and other means and rehabilitating addicted individuals.[22]

One characteristic of severely distressed neighborhoods is a dearth of middle-class residents who, in other neighborhoods, provide support for stable employment and other positive behavior:

> One key source of the decline in social capital in many urban neighborhoods has been the suburbanization of the American middle class. When better-educated, employed persons in intact families move from a neighborhood, they take social capital with them. . . . The proportion of inner-city residents who are employed has fallen, undermining their incomes and reducing financial support for neighborhood institutions, weakening norms favoring employment, and eliminating social contacts for job seeking.[23]

To rebuild the influence of positive role models in inner-city communities, CED has advocated changes in housing policies (such as eligibility rules for public housing projects) that would reduce the isolation of low-income families and mix them with middle-class neighbors. Another effective approach to the same problem involves mentoring programs that provide contact between inner-city youth and stably employed role models, many of them from outside the young people's home communities.[24] *

---

22. *Rebuilding Inner-City Communities,* pp. 5-6.

23. *Rebuilding Inner-City Communities,* p. 16.

24. *Rebuilding Inner-City Communities,* p. 56; see also *Strengthening Social Infrastructure for Successful Teenage Development and Transition to Adulthood* (Philadelphia: Public/Private Ventures, 1993).

---

*See memorandum by PETER A. BENOLIEL, (page 31).

Finally, CED has noted a fundamental flaw in many inner-city initiatives: their tendency to impose solutions on distressed neighborhoods rather than develop solutions jointly with the residents of these neighborhoods. Such efforts have limited sustainability because they are not part of the community fabric, may not reflect local priorities, and fail to attract the support of those persons most directly affected. The efforts also represent lost opportunities to strengthen leadership organizations within the distressed communities that can serve as rallying points and organizing vehicles for addressing other problems in these multiply troubled neighborhoods. Therefore, in educational and employment initiatives, as well as other efforts to improve inner-city communities:

> The public sector should routinely consult community-based organizations on decisions affecting their neighborhoods; join *ad hoc* coalitions with community groups to implement specific projects; participate in ongoing partnerships that bring together the public, business, philanthropic, and community sectors; and require collaborative planning and nongovernmental matching for publicly funded initiatives. [It]. . . should aggressively seek opportunities to employ community-based organizations as front-line implementers of public initiatives. For example, government agencies should increasingly contract with community-based organizations to deliver publicly funded services. . . . Sustained community building occurs primarily through ongoing institutions such as community development corporations, schools, and churches. . . . Public funds should be used to enhance the institutional strength of community-based institutions.[25]

---

25. *Rebuilding Inner-City Communities*, pp. 6-7. See also *The Path of Most Resistance, Reflections on Lessons Learned from New Futures* (Baltimore, Md.: Annie E. Casey Foundation, no date).

STRENGTHENING THE NATION'S ELEMENTARY AND SECONDARY SCHOOLS

The previous section emphasized the role of the community in supporting education and the ways in which an inner-city environment can hamper education and employment. Nonetheless, overemphasis on these issues can distract attention from changes needed in schools themselves. However difficult their operating environments, schools remain responsible for educating their students efficiently and effectively. Indeed, in many inner-city neighborhoods, public schools represent virtually the only educational resource for their students, in contrast with suburban communities, where middle-class students have family and institutional alternatives that can substitute for deficient services provided by schools.

How can inner-city schools fulfill these responsibilities? How can they more effectively prepare their students for the world of work?

Connecting entry-level workers to career employment cannot be accomplished simply by improving the placement process that occurs at graduation. By themselves, classes in the final year of high school that teach résumé preparation and job-interviewing skills are not sufficient. Instead, improvements are required in the learning process from kindergarten through grade twelve.

CED believes that school reform must begin with high standards for student achievement. Even in affluent suburban schools, there is often too little emphasis on the value of learning, limited orientation toward long-term goals, and lack of peer support for studying. In inner-city schools, peer pressure may be particularly discouraging to student achievement.[26] To counter such pressures CED advocates that:

26. Signithia Fordham and John Ogbu, "Black Students' School Success: Coping with the Burden of Acting White," *Urban Review* 18 (1986): 176-206.

The first priority of those who govern education should be to establish learning and achievement as the primary missions of the schools. . . . They should set rigorous content and performance standards that clearly indicate what students should know and be able to do. . . . This policy shift will help those at the school level to develop rigorous academic curricula, indicate areas where schools need to improve, and send the message that society expects high academic achievement.[27]

Strengthening the quality and preparation of teachers is also central to the improvement of school performance:

CED recommends that hiring criteria for high school teachers place more emphasis on preparation and demonstrated mastery in subjects they teach. Teacher compensation should reward improvements in student performance and be sufficiently flexible to relieve shortages of qualified teachers in important subjects.[28]

CED also recommends that schools dramatically increase their use of information technology to increase teachers' skills and knowledge and raise students' achievement:

America's schools should move ahead as quickly as possible to integrate information technologies into classroom instruction and curricula. We recommend the following strategies: Improve professional development for teachers. . . . Increase availability of computers in the classroom. . . . Increase access to information technology for low-income children. . . . Make the Internet and other parts of the National Information Infrastructure more accessible to schools . . . . Expand federal support for school technology initiatives.[29]

---

27. *Putting Learning First,* pp. 3-4.

28. *American Workers and Economic Change,* p. 47.

29. *Connecting Students to a Changing World: A Technology Strategy for Improving Mathematics and Science Education*(New York: Committee for Economic Development, 1995), pp. xi-xiv.

To achieve these goals, CED advocates revamping the governance and management of schools to emphasize incentives for results rather than compliance with rules and regulations. We believe that this would result in:

> . . . an education system that rewards success from the classroom up rather than top-down compliance. We urge experimentation with new approaches that define and reward performance. Specifically, we continue to advocate *site-based management* in which teachers, administrators, parents, and students have both more authority and more accountability. . . . We advocate *charter schools* (publicly funded schools designed and run under performance-based contracts). . . . We also strongly support a vigorous expansion of *public school choice.*[30]

RETHINKING STYLES OF TEACHING AND LEARNING

Implementation of these recommendations would significantly improve the performance of America's schools, especially in inner-city communities. However, even these changes would not fully address the inadequacies in students' preparation for the world of work. Unless schools also implement changes in pedagogy — in how students and teachers spend their days in the classroom — many of the deficiencies of the nation's schools will persist. School reform must challenge educators to reexamine some of their fundamental assumptions about teaching and learning.

The primary motivation for this reexamination is the failure of contemporary schools to engage the interest and energy of large numbers of their students. This problem is revealed most dramatically in rates of school dropouts as high as 80 percent in some distressed neighborhoods.[31] A less dramatic form of the same problem is more universal: A substantial number of students, from inner cities to affluent suburbs, sleepwalk through

---

30. *American Workers and Economic Change*, pp. 46-47. See also *Putting Learning First.*

31. *Rebuilding Inner-City Communities*, p. 12.

their school years and graduate with limited skills. This problem may affect as many as three out of four of the nation's students in varying degrees.[32]

As experienced teachers well know, unmotivated students are difficult to teach, but engaged students often reach impressive levels of educational achievement even in adverse circumstances. Schools must give priority to capturing the attention of their students. To do so, they must provide an answer to the recurrent question: "Why should we bother to learn this?"

A second reason for changing styles of teaching and learning is to reach the broad range of students who make up today's diverse student bodies. Many modes of instruction common in the nation's classrooms, such as lectures on abstract concepts, effectively communicate to only a minority of students. They are often particularly ineffective for students with gaps in their educational preparation or limited command of English. Equally, they are often mismatched with students whose most effective learning styles are not aural and abstract.[33]

The rising technological demands of the workplace make such failures increasingly unacceptable. To prosper in the workplace of the future, *all* students need advanced academic skills: mathematics at the level of algebra and beyond, facility with modern information technology, comprehension of complex written material, and articulate written and oral communication. In former decades, schools might have been considered satisfactory if they taught such subjects to college-bound students and graduated others with more modest skills from classes in "basic math" and "practical English." That level of school performance is no longer adequate.

Fortunately, innovative pedagogy now makes advanced academic material accessible to a broad range of students. Belatedly articulating principles that excellent teachers have long known intuitively, cognitive science concludes that most learners best grasp concepts through examples and hands-on manipulation. It also argues that intelligence has multiple dimensions, so that diverse learning styles should be used to present

---

32. At the CED/MetLife Symposium on December 5, 1995, estimates ranging from 50 percent to 80 percent were suggested by such experts as William Spring, James Clark, and John Bishop.

33. Howard Gardener, *Frames of Mind: A Theory of Multiple Intelligences* (New York: Basic Books, 1983).

lessons. When such insights are reflected in classroom practices, the range of students achieving levels of learning thought feasible only for the "college bound" increases dramatically.[34]

A final motivation for rethinking styles of teaching and learning is to remove the conflict between classroom practices and the habits and skills valued in the workplace. The typical style of teaching and learning in today's elementary and secondary schools contrasts starkly with the patterns of work that students experience when they become employees. School often features rote memory and regurgitation, teachers treated as unbending authorities, students competing rather than cooperating, and problems that have single or simple answers. The modern workplace, however, increasingly emphasizes skills in seeking information, supervisors as coaches, employees working in teams, and complex, unstructured problems. Schools need to avoid teaching students 12 years of work habits antithetical to those they will need after graduation. Instead, they need to make the mastery of workplace competencies and the development of appropriate work attitudes explicit educational objectives.[35]

THE CONTEXTUALIZED CLASSROOM

The central concept of this new approach to teaching is *contextualization*, presenting abstract concepts in a motivating context.[36] This approach does

---

34. Susan Berryman, *Cognitive Science: Indicting Today's Schools and Designing Effective Learning Environments* (Washington, D.C.: U.S. Department of Labor, 1991); Senta A. Raizen, *Reforming Education for Work: A Cognitive Science Perspective* (Berkeley, Calif.: National Center for Research in Vocational Education, 1989); Robert Crain, Amy Heebner, and Yui-Pong Si, *The Effectiveness of New York City's Career Magnet Schools: An Evaluation of Ninth Grade Performance Using an Experimental Design* (Berkeley, Calif.: National Center for Research in Vocational Education, 1992).

35. *What Work Requires of Schools: A SCANS Report for America 2000* (Washington, D.C.: U.S. Department of Labor, 1991). See also *Investing in Our Children: Business and the Public Schools,* Chapter 2.

36. W. Norton Grubb, *Learning to Work: The Case for Reintegrating Job Training and Education* (New York: Russell Sage Foundation, 1996); Nancy Adelman, *The Case for Integration of Academic and Vocational Education* (Washington, D.C.: Policy Studies Associates, 1989); Thomas Bailey, *Changes in the Nature and Structure of Work: Implications for Skill Requirements and Skill Formation* (New York: Columbia University, 1990); John Bishop, *Expertise and Excellence* (Ithaca, N.Y.: Cornell University Center for Advanced Human Resource Studies, 1995); Richard Kazis, *Improving the Transition from School to Work in the United States* (Washington, D.C.: American Youth Policy Forum, 1993); and Basil Whiting, *Improving the Transition from School to Work* (Kansas City, MO.: Ewing Marion Kauffman Foundation, 1994).

not mean watering down academic content. Instead, it means motivating a broad range of students to master advanced academic content by demonstrating that the concepts are connected with their lives and interests.

Here is how the concept is implemented in a partnership between the District of Columbia's public schools and a nonprofit organization, Funds for the Community's Future:

> Starting at an early age, students need to have their classroom lessons inextricably linked to something that they experience and that they do. So in science class, an experiment in the lab should be followed by a project in the neighborhood. It all starts with kids because they should help determine the project that interests them in the first place.
>
> Lead paint is a concern of some students after recent public- awareness campaigns. So if you are a science teacher and you find this to be true in your class, the class should learn an experiment to test for lead paint, and they should do the tests on houses that surround their school. Then the history and English classes should research and write a pamphlet about the issue of lead paint. Then the printing class can take the information, lay it out, and print a pamphlet. Students can present what they have done to local neighborhood associations and distribute this information to their community.
>
> Then the classes can go on a field trip to a local company that employs scientists to show the students what these scientists are working on. They should go on a field trip to a printing company to show that there are career opportunities there as well. . . . There should be internships for students of working age who have been through these classes and who know how to conduct experiments.[37]

37. Remarks of David Milner, President, Funds for the Community's Future, at the CED/MetLife Symposium, December 5, 1995. Throughout this policy statement, quotations from this symposium have been edited for clarity.

As this example demonstrates, contextualization frequently uses the workplace as part or all of the motivating context. This practice makes sense because of the direct connection to the world of work and the explicitness of messages concerning the payoffs for academic achievement. It is particularly useful for inner-city students, whose home environments often provide less exposure to the world of work than occurs routinely via family and neighbors in middle-class neighborhoods.

For models of work-contextualized learning, educational innovators often point to a long-neglected part of the nation's educational system: vocational education.[38] In recent decades, vocational education has often consisted largely of shop classes that primarily enroll students considered ineducable or unruly. Yet, in other times and places, the workplace-oriented, hands-on style of instruction in vocational education has produced students both skilled and smart. Effective work-contextualized schools merge the *learning methods* of vocational education with the *content* of academic education.

The result is a classroom that does not look at all like the traditional shop class. For instance, consider the emerging shape of vocational education in the Milwaukee Public Schools:

The new vocational education is now in 23 elementary schools, 10 middle schools, and 8 high schools. We are focusing on actively involving students in business and work-site experiences:

- From elementary school students visiting a neighborhood manufacturer where they are given actual company problems, using their math skills and problem-solving skills, in the manufacturer's training room

- To another elementary school that has a student-run bank, through the cooperation and training of a local bank, in which students interview for positions

38. See W. Norton Grubb et al., *The Cunning Hand, The Cultured Mind: Models for Integrating Academic and Vocational Education* (Berkeley, Calif.: National Center for Research in Vocational Education, 1991); Vernay Mitchell, *Exemplary Urban Career-Oriented Secondary School Programs* (Berkeley, Calif.: National Center for Research in Vocational Education, 1990); Susan Bodilly et al., *Integrating Academic and Vocational Education: Lessons from Eight Early Innovators* (Santa Monica, Calif.: RAND, 1993); and W. Norton Grubb, ed., *Education Through Occupations in the American High School* (New York: Teachers College Press, 1995).

- To a middle school involved in an electronic plant in which employers spend time in the classroom with students, spend time developing the math and science curriculum, and have students involved in various work phases at the plant

- To a high school that developed a close relationship with the Milwaukee Department of City Development, involving students in various fields of city planning — architecture, engineering, media, and event planning. Students developed a plan for the Economic Committee of the Common Council and talked to our mayor. As a result, 14 students had summer jobs in city offices.

We want every student in our district, from elementary through high school, to be exposed to career opportunities.[39]

Seeking similar goals in its work with 450 schools in 22 states, the Southern Regional Education Board operates around three principles:

The first one is to raise expectations because we know students won't exceed our expectations.

The second one is to put more theory — math, science, language arts — in the vocational classes.

The third one is to put more applications into math, science, and language arts classes.

In other words, teach every concept with an application the students can buy into. When students buy into it, they learn, they are interested in learning, and teachers become enthusiastic because they are encouraged.[40]

Such methods of linking the workplace and the classroom are gradually moving from exotic experiments to accepted educational practice. Some

39. Remarks by Eve Hall, Executive Assistant to the Superintendent, Milwaukee Public Schools, at the CED/MetLife Symposium, December 5, 1995.

40. Remarks of James Clark, Southern Regional Education Board, at the CED/MetLife Symposium, December 5, 1995.

of these innovations have been initiated by local school districts. Others have been sparked by federal initiatives, particularly under the Carl D. Perkins Vocational and Applied Technology Education Act of 1990 and the School-to-Work Opportunities Act of 1994. These model initiatives commonly emphasize the following:[41]

- Integration of academic and vocational education, using the world of work as a motivating context for academic learning.

- Coordination of secondary school and post-secondary education through "tech prep" and "2+2" programs. Under these programs, the final two years of high school and two years in a community college or vocational school form a continuous educational experience.

- Exposure of students, teachers, and school counselors to the world of work through guest speakers, field visits, job shadowing, and work internships.

- Design of classroom activities to develop workplace competencies and work attitudes.

- Utilization of students' summer jobs and after-school jobs as venues for learning. Job supervisors and teachers work together to identify the educational needs of individual student-workers, design skill development activities that occur in the workplace, and develop classroom activities that enhance on-the-job competencies.

- Organization of high schools into "academies," "schools-within-a-school," or "majors" centered around careers and industries.

- Integration of career awareness and career exploration into the curriculum throughout the elementary and middle-school years.[42]

- Expansion of opportunities for worksite-based learning through internships, cooperative education, and apprenticeships.

---

41. Marc Bendick, Jr., "Linking Learning and Earning," *Economic Development Quarterly* (Fall, 1996), pp. 217-223.

42. It is crucial to begin using contextualization to engage student interest early in their school careers because the process of disengagement and disaffection from education and work can begin as early as the elementary school years. See *Educational Reforms and Students at Risk, A Review of the Current State of the Art*, Robert Rossi and Alesia Montgomery, eds. (Washington, D.C.: U.S. Department of Education, 1994).

The main deficiency of these initiatives is their small scale. For example, among the 17 million students in the nation's secondary schools, "tech prep" enrolls only about 50,000 and career academies only 10,000.[43]

CED recommends that such innovations in curricula and pedagogy be continued and expanded. We urge school districts to adopt them for all students not only for "vocational" students or students in inner-city schools. We counsel federal and state governments to continue to support them with funds and leadership. And we encourage employers to continue their support, particularly through site visits, guest speakers, work internships, curriculum advice, and other activities where what employers provide cannot readily be obtained from other sources.

---

43. Bailey, *Changes in the Nature and Structure of Work.*

EMPLOYMENT PRACTICES TO COMPLEMENT SCHOOL REFORMS

Work-contextualized schools can produce young people ready for the world of work. But the full benefits of improved student preparation will be realized only when changes in the workplace complement and reinforce those in the classroom. For inner-city youth to be connected effectively to career employment, employers must modify the ways they interact with young job seekers and entry-level employees.

EXPANDING METHODS OF EMPLOYEE RECRUITMENT

One constraint on job opportunities for inner-city youth is the distance between the neighborhoods where they live and locations where jobs are concentrated. In the Washington, D.C. metropolitan area, for example, two out of three job openings are located in the suburbs, as many as 25 miles away from the central city and in locations perceived as inaccessible and hostile by many inner-city job seekers.[44]

Some employers address this problem by placing plants and offices in inner-city locations. Because these facilities may provide jobs that are locally accessible to inner-city residents, they may be particularly important for students seeking part-time employment and entry-level workers who may not have access to automobiles.[45] However, inner-city locations are not an option for many other firms, and it is by no means the only way to open jobs to inner-city residents. Like the vast majority of workers in American

---

44. Marc Bendick, Jr., and Mary Lou Egan, *Jobs: Employment Opportunities in the Washington Metropolitan Area for Persons with Limited Employment Qualifications* (Washington, D.C.: Greater Washington Research Center, 1988), pp. 17-19. See also Keith Ihlanfeldt, *Job Accessibility and the Employment and School Enrollment of Teenagers* (Kalamazoo, Mich.: Upjohn Institute for Employment Research, 1992), and Harry Holzer, "Black Unemployment Problems: New Evidence, Old Questions," *Journal of Policy Analysis and Management* 13 (1994): 699-722.

45. *Rebuilding Inner-City Communities*, pp. 50-53; George Galster and Sean Killen, "The Geography of Metropolitan Opportunity," *Housing Policy Debate* 6,(no. 1, 1995): 43.

society, many employed residents of inner cities can commute to jobs outside their neighborhoods. But the migration of employment to the suburbs has severed many of the networks through which job seekers find out about employment opportunities and employers receive informal information about applicants.[46] To offset this loss, CED urges renewed efforts by employers to build recruiting relationships in inner-city neighborhoods.

With proper support, employers can be convinced to participate in such ventures. Consider, for instance, Boston's experience with employer involvement:

> We got the private sector to organize work opportunities after school, in the summer, and upon graduation. We got real scale. We have 3,300 summer jobs. We have unemployment for our high school graduates down to 4 percent. How did we do it? We have a model in which the better angels of the private sector can be coaxed to the table because we provide support for employers who agree to give our kids a shot.
>
> It turns out that these kids, while they do not have all the requisite skills, are wonderful kids, 80 or 90 percent of them. But there is the question of getting them in the shop. We have a career specialist in each high school who is a coach. You have to know the kids and know the employers. Employers want a reliable intermediary much more than they want incentives.[47]

This approach appropriately emphasizes the role of personal referrals in helping employers screen job applicants. To avoid a volume of applicants they fear will not be qualified, employers often closely guard information about job openings. Rather than publicly advertise, they seek applicants through current employees and other personal contacts. In these circumstances, young workers with a network of employed, well-placed family, friends, and neighbors have substantial advantages over their equally qualified peers without such relationships.

---

46. In *Rebuilding Inner-City Communities*, Chapter 2, CED discusses these networks as part of *social capital* (see footnote 16).

47. Remarks by William Spring, Vice President, Federal Reserve Bank of Boston, at the CED/MetLife Symposium, December 5, 1995.

Employers can offset this handicap by developing personal contacts with referral sources that are in touch with inner-city job seekers. In particular, they can form relationships with teachers and counselors in inner-city schools, as well as with community institutions such as churches, boys and girls clubs, and community development corporations.[48] In many cases, these relationships can develop through employers' participation in work-contextualized schools, as a by-product of the site visits and guest speaker activities discussed earlier in this statement.

Student internships, summer jobs, and part-time jobs represent other important ways to enhance employment opportunities for inner-city youth. These arrangements allow employers to get to know students as individuals and to judge their performance in actual work situations, thereby overcoming stereotypes that lead some employers to avoid these persons when they apply for employment without prior relationships.[49]

A third approach that enhances opportunities for inner-city youth with limited personal networks is for employers to advertise job vacancies publicly, for example, in newspapers or through the public employment service. In the American labor market today, about two thirds of all job openings, especially better-quality, career-oriented positions, are never publicly advertised.[50]

To make open advertising more feasible, however, employers need to be able to screen a large volume of applicants rapidly. That process would be facilitated if current legal constraints on the use of diplomas and high school grades as screening criteria were reduced.[51]

---

48. *Rebuilding Inner-City Communities*, pp. 20-21. See also Bennett Harrison, *Building Bridges: Community Development Corporations and the World of Employment Training* (New York: Ford Foundation, 1995), Chapter 2.

49. Young African-American and Hispanic job seekers encounter discrimination approximately 25 percent of the time they apply for entry-level employment, and this rate is even higher for jobs in the suburbs. See Marc Bendick, Jr., et al., "Measuring Employment Discrimination Through Controlled Experiments," *Review of Black Political Economy* 23 (Summer 1994): 25-48. See also Joleen Neckerman and Kathryn Kirschenman, " 'We'd Love to Hire Them, But...The Meaning of Race for Employers," in *The Urban Underclass*, ed. Christopher Jencks and Paul E. Peterson (Washington, D.C.: The Brookings Institution, 1991), pp. 203-234, and *Rebuilding Inner-City Communities*, pp. 17, 54.

50. Marc Bendick, Jr., "Matching Workers and Job Opportunities: What Role for the Federal-State Employment Service?" in *Rethinking Employment Policy*, ed. D. Bawden and F. Skidmore (Washington, D.C.: Urban Institute Press, 1989), pp. 81-108. See also Harry Holzer, *What Employers Want: Job Prospects for Less-Educated Workers* (New York: Russell Sage Foundation, 1996).

51. Before high school graduation or grade averages can be legally used to screen job applicants, these criteria often must be demonstrated to be job-related predictors of performance in the entry-level jobs being filled. Although this requirement is intended to offer protection against hiring discrimination, it reduces incentives to invest in the education necessary to move beyond entry-level positions. Declaring that a high school diploma or minimum grade average is automatically job related for all jobs would restore those incentives. See *American Workers and Economic Change*, p. 12.

MAKING SCHOOL ACHIEVEMENT PAY

Students are constantly told that "education pays." That maxim proves true in the long run and for major differences in educational credentials. For example, on average, college graduates earn substantially more over their working lives than high school graduates. However, the initial personal experiences of many entry-level workers contradict the maxim. Major earnings differences between high school dropouts and high school graduates and between students who studied advanced subjects and those who merely skimmed by do not appear for many entry-level workers until they are in their mid-twenties.[52]

Such a pattern is to be expected if the initial skill requirements of many entry-level jobs are limited and wages are based only on current productivity. However, many young workers have short time horizons. Consequently, short-term signals are crucial for keeping them on a career-productive track. Wages that do not reflect workers' qualifications for future productivity dampen incentives for educational effort and hamper a firm's retention of employees with greater long-run potential. CED urges employers to rethink wage policies in order to differentiate among entry-level workers with the same current duties but different levels of educational accomplishment.[53]

The same principle can be applied to hiring decisions: In selecting among entry-level job applicants, employers should give preference to those who enrolled in tougher school subjects, demonstrated better attendance, earned higher grades, and acquired more work-relevant skills.

To do so, of course, requires that employers have detailed information on students' educational accomplishments. Today, employers seldom request high school transcripts or solicit recommendations from high school

---

52. Joseph Altonji, "The Effects of High School Curriculum on Education and Labor Market Outcomes," *Journal of Human Resources* 30 (1995): pp. 409-438; Henry Farber and Robert Gibbons, *Learning and Wage Dynamics* (Princeton, N.J.: Princeton University Industrial Relations Section, 1994); John D. Owen, *Why Our Kids Don't Study: An Economist's Perspective* (Baltimore, Md.: Johns Hopkins University Press, 1995).

53. To be most effective, these wage differences should be based on specific skills rather than credentials such as high school diplomas. However, skills should not be valued narrowly. The goal is to create short-run payoffs for productivity differences that manifest themselves primarily in the long run. Academic fundamentals, which support flexibility and acquisition of future skills, should be rewarded more than skills that rapidly become obsolete. For instance, mastery of algebra should command a greater wage differential than knowledge of a currently popular computer program. See John L. Morris, "Lessons Learned in Skill-Based Pay," *HR Magazine* (June 1996): 136-142.

teachers.[54] **CED urges employers to incorporate information on student performance, such as that contained in high school transcripts and teacher recommendations, into their entry-level hiring decisions.*** We also urge **employers to work with schools to develop additional means of documenting student achievement, including improved standardized tests, certificates of skill achievement, and portfolios of students' work.**[55]

MAXIMIZING THE PRODUCTIVITY OF
A DIVERSE WORKFORCE

When young persons are hired from inner-city neighborhoods, they join company work forces that are becoming increasingly diverse in gender, age, race, ethnicity, and other personal characteristics. Diverse work groups are often more open and creative in their decision making and better able to relate to diverse customers in both domestic and international markets. CED believes that valuing diversity is a good business practice and recommends that American employers invest in training and communications programs to manage these diverse work forces more effectively.[56] In addition to their more general benefits, such initiatives can help companies to retain and utilize young inner-city employees more efficiently.

In terms of employment opportunities for young inner-city workers, entry-level positions requiring limited skills should represent only a starting point. In effect, many workplaces today divide employees into castes based on their precareer education. Employees who acquire further education while they work often experience little evolution in their duties as their classes enhance their capabilities; and when they complete college degrees, they often face resistance to breaking into professional ranks. Such treatment contradicts the reality that lifelong learning, including more persons attending school while working and more employees undergoing retraining to combat obsolescence, is increasingly the norm in the Ameri-

---

54. John Bishop, "High School Performance and Employee Recruitment," *Journal of Labor Research* 13 (1992): 41-44; Secretary's Commission on Achieving Necessary Skills, *Learning a Living,* Chapter 6.

55. *American Workers and Economic Change,* p. 12; *Putting Learning First,* pp. 24-25.

56. *American Workers and Economic Change,* p. 50. See also Susan E. Jackson and Associates, *Diversity in the Workplace* (New York: Guilford Press, 1992) and R. Roosevelt Thomas, "From Affirmative Action to Managing Diversity," *Harvard Business Review* (March-April 1990): 107-117.

---

*See memorandum by PETER A. BENOLIEL, (page 31).

can economy.[57] When employers base opportunities for advancement less on employees' histories and more on current skills, workers have incentives to acquire and maintain the competencies that productivity increasingly requires.

These circumstances affect all workers, but they are particularly relevant to young inner-city employees. Although postsecondary education is increasingly required for quality career employment, many inner-city youths require some work experience before they understand that message. Therefore, CED urges employers to encourage and facilitate continuing education for entry-level workers, as well as other workers, and reward employees' educational investments with opportunities to advance.[58]

ENHANCING PATHS FOR UPWARD MOBILITY

There are well-established terms, of course, for arrangements that advance employees as their experience and skills grow: career paths and job ladders. Although such paths are common in many American workplaces, they are inaccessible to many young workers from the inner city because the level of experience, skills, and maturity required for initial positions on these paths is higher than many of these workers possess. Those hired for initial career-path positions are often in their early to middle twenties with some postsecondary education and work experience.[59] With resources and an understanding of careers, many middle-class youths accumulate these prerequisites on their own. However, many of their inner-city counterparts are unlikely to do so unless their early job experience *directly* links them to career positions. CED urges employers to restructure entry-level employment to increase opportunities for entry into career paths at age 18 rather than 25.

Here is how educational consultant Basil Whiting describes Workplus, an initiative assisting firms to treat entry-level workers in the context of long-term careers:

---

57. *An America That Works*, Chapters 4 and 5.

58. *American Workers and Economic Change*, pp. 34-37.

59. Robert Zemsky, *What Employers Want: Employer Perspectives on Youth, the Youth Labor Market, and Prospects for a National System of Youth Apprenticeship* (Philadelphia, Pa.: National Center on the Educational Quality of the Workforce, University of Pennsylvania, 1994); Holzer, *What Employers Want*.

The existing youth labor market has 6 million kids from 16 to 25 working in a "secondary labor market." They lily-pad hop from job to job in search of a little money, but nothing stable. To make that a more developmentally effective experience, you have to add mechanisms to make it more orderly.

McDonald's is one of the best-managed corporations in the country and does an extraordinary job. At the age of 18, they'll tell you, "If you apply yourself, at 22 or so, you can be an assistant store manager making $25,000 to $30,000 or more a year." That is not bad for a kid these days. McDonald's, however, is not the common employer.

Workplus is involved with employers of these kinds of kids in these kinds of jobs. We train supervisors to be more effective, to enable young workers to be effective workers, and to be career-guided. We structure this labor market to help kids move from job to job in some purposeful way and to supplement their work experience with education and other services. We move them through a sequence of jobs that allows them to accumulate a résumé that commends itself to future employers.[60]

To pursue the same objectives, some employers have considered expanded use of apprenticeships, which combine continuing education with work and lead to recognized credentials. In the American labor market, apprenticeships have been applied primarily in a limited range of crafts, such as carpentry or plumbing. However, in nations such as Germany, the same concept is applied to a much broader range of manufacturing, office, and service occupations.[61] **CED recommends that expanded use of formal apprenticeships be considered. This approach would enhance the developmental content of early work experience and expand the range of occupations with explicit paths of upward mobility.**

60. Remarks of Basil Whiting, Public/Private Ventures, at the CED/MetLife Symposium, December 5, 1995. For other examples, see Keith MacAllum and Patricia Ma, *Skills, Standards, and Entry-Level Work* (Washington, D.C.: U.S. Department of Labor, 1995), p. 34, and Mary Lou Egan and Marc Bendick, Jr., *Managing Greater Washington's Changing Work Force: Keys to Productivity and Profit* (Washington, D.C.: Greater Washington Research Center, 1991), pp. 34-36.

61. Lerman, "The Compelling Case"; Lerman, "Building Hope, Skills, and Careers"; *Real Jobs for Real People, An Employer's Guide to Youth Apprenticeships* (Washington, D.C.: National Alliance of Business, 1992); Paul Osterman, "Involving Employers in School-to-Work Programs," in *Learning to Work, Employer Involvement in School-to-Work Transition Programs*, ed. Thomas Bailey (Washington, D.C.: The Brookings Institution, 1995), pp. 75-87.

THE SCHOOL/EMPLOYER/ PUBLIC POLICY PARTNERSHIP

Preparing America's youth for employment is a national investment. Even in times of concern about the federal deficit, adequate funding for education and education-to-work transition should receive high priority. In particular, CED supports:

> ... special efforts to improve the quality of public education in less affluent school districts, including the provision of adequate funding in those situations where it is lacking. We should also provide adequate public support for qualified and motivated students of limited means to pursue postsecondary education.[62]

The approaches described in this statement can be dividend-paying investments for the business community as well as the public sector. To mobilize employer support, it is not necessary to appeal only to business's sense of social responsibility. If restructured personnel practices in combination with strengthened schools produce more capable employees, jobs need not be "dumbed down," shortages of skilled workers can be avoided, expensive turnover can be slowed, and employers can obtain higher returns on their investments in technology and equipment. Thus, employers can enhance their production efficiency, competitiveness, and profitability.

Treating these initiatives as investments and demonstrating their payoffs are important in obtaining business cooperation. As Harry P. Kamen, Chairman, President and Chief Executive Officer of the Metropolitan Life Insurance Company, stated in his keynote address at the CED/MetLife symposium:

---

62. *American Workers and Economic Change*, p. 49.

There is one good way to recruit a business partner: Invite him to share in your success. . . . I would say to our schools: Don't just tell us you need internships; show us your plan for changing students' lives through internships. Don't just ask us to sponsor a career-awareness program; show us how that will complete your plan for launching careers. Don't emphasize your needs; show us also your strengths. . . . Let's look for opportunities to ignite the spark of success in schools. That will make businesses seize the opportunity to invest in a promising partnership.[63]

This program statement identifies numerous opportunities for such promising partnerships.

---

63. Remarks of Harry P. Kamen, Metropolitan Life Insurance Company, at the CED/MetLife Symposium, December 5, 1995.

MEMORANDA OF COMMENT, RESERVATION, OR DISSENT

Page 10, PETER A. BENOLIEL

I am uncomfortable with the notion denigrating the value of "problems that have single...answers." In learning mathematics, algebra, trigonometry, geometry, and calculus problems more often than not have single, correct answers; similarly the case with the study of the physical and life sciences at the more basic levels. Students must undergo that discipline if higher standards of expectation and outcome is our goal.

Page 26, PETER A. BENOLIEL

This is a particularly important recommendation as it carries with it certain collateral benefits — i.e., the potentiality of mentoring and networking relationships, a partial substitute for the social capital so absent from many young peoples' lives.

OBJECTIVES OF THE COMMITTEE FOR ECONOMIC DEVELOPMENT

For more than 50 years, the Committee for Economic Development has been a respected influence on the formation of business and public policy. CED is devoted to these two objectives:

To develop, through objective research and informed discussion, findings and recommendations for private and public policy that will contribute to preserving and strengthening our free society, achieving steady economic growth at high employment and reasonably stable prices, increasing productivity and living standards, providing greater and more equal opportunity for every citizen, and improving the quality of life for all.

To bring about increasing understanding by present and future leaders in business, government, and education, and among concerned citizens of the importance of these objectives and the ways in which they can be achieved.

CED's work is supported by private voluntary contributions from business and industry, foundations, and individuals. It is independent, nonprofit, nonpartisan, and nonpolitical.

Through this business-academic partnership, CED endeavors to develop policy statements and other research materials that commend themselves as guides to public and business policy; that can be used as texts in college economics and political science courses and in management training courses; that will be considered and discussed by newspaper and magazine editors, columnists, and commentators; and that are distributed abroad to promote better understanding of the American economic system.

CED believes that by enabling business leaders to demonstrate constructively their concern for the general welfare, it is helping business to earn and maintain the national and community respect essential to the successful functioning of the free enterprise capitalist system.